KAMA SUTRA

THE ANCIENT ART OF MAKING LOVE

by

Madelyn Carol Fajardo

Publisher

Attar Incorporated
Westlake Village, California

Acknowledgements

Dedicated to the memory of Hal Hauser, aka Hal Captain, co-founder of the Kama Sutra Company. Many thanks to his partner, Joe Bolstad, for his continued efforts to bring couples closer together.

The poetic descriptions of the positions by Helga Kollar, MA, and her delightful story, have brought the Ancient Art of Kama Sutra into a romantic context for contemporary couples.

Much appreciation to Mark Bloom for his ability to provide the historical background which has given the book a richer perspective.

Attar Incorporated
2260 Townsgate Road Suite 3
Westlake Village, CA 91361
Library of Congress catalogue card number 98-93932
ISBN 0-9668398-0-3
Printed in Hong Kong

Letter from the Author

It has been nearly thirty years since I began working for the Kama Sutra Company, and over ten since my journeys into India began. I became fascinated with Indian culture and food, but most of all with the people. Many seemed to be the simplest, poorest, and yet the happiest people I have ever known. Quite an amazing and interesting achievement. Even though the journey to India is long and hard, I always return with a new zest for life. My research on the *Kama Sutra* began as I traveled through India. I was able to acquire writings and original hand paintings of various love garden settings, romantic embraces, and, much to my delight, many of the love making positions, all presented in a most beautiful format. They inspired me to put together a book which would be both an informative and romantic love manual—a piece that would inspire lovers to take time for each other. Have an evening of inspiration—create the setting with a selection of scents, flowers, oils, lotions and creams. Select the music to be played. Find the space and the time to practice "The Ancient Art of Making Love."

I hope all who read this book will enjoy. Wishing you love and happiness.

Madelyn

Kama is the consciousness of pleasure

that arises from the contact

of the five senses of hearing, feeling,

seeing, tasting and smelling,

assisted by the mind

together with the soul . . .

INTRODUCTION

Since the beginning of civilization, ideas about love making have been questioned and become diversified in every culture. What one group of people finds to be perfectly acceptable is deemed sorely incorrect by another. Individuals within each culture frequently have opposing views as well. It is unlikely that there will ever be anything approaching a global consensus on appropriate sexual practices.

The word *kama* means desire, and it includes all other words pertaining to desire such as love and affection. In Hinduism, *kama* also refers to the god of love and desire. *Sutra* means aphorisms, principles, or rules. Consequently, *Kama Sutra* may be translated as *The Aphorisms of Love*. Nearly two thousand years ago, an erudite sage named Vatsayayana had compiled from ancient sources Hindu dogma on the subject of sexology. Far from being lascivious and pornographic, as judged by the Western mind, these works still represent a wealth of information on the history, philosophy, social customs, and scientific inquiry of a complex culture. With sensitivity and decorum, the text is embellished with depictions of erotic embraces by notable artists from various schools of painting.

While much of the *Kama Sutra* is about different positions of sexual union, also known as sexual congress, Vatsayayana's work details much of what takes place before and afterwards. Much of this information is intended to enhance sexual experience or improve the power of attraction. The subjects addressed in Vatsayayana's *Kama Sutra* include:

    1. **The life of a citizen**, which concerns personal hygiene, putting on perfumes and oils to attract others, eating properly, having appropriate clothing and jewelry, and having social

gatherings.

2. **Embracing, kissing, and marking or scratching with nails**. Discussed in great detail, there are many names for different types of embraces, kisses, and scratching—each one with its own particular purpose depending upon the situation (such as how well the two people know each other). While marking and scratching are done primarily before sexual congress, Vatsayayana tends to emphasize the notion that there are no guidelines in making love.

3. **Seduction**. This section comprises much of Vatsayayana's work. He breaks down characteristics of men and women, describing which men will gain women's affection and the reasons why a woman might reject a man. Many of the qualities he lists are considered desirable in the Western world as well— good looks, confidence, intelligence, etc. Other verses examine a woman's mind and methods of enticement to win her over.

4. **Marriage**. The work addresses both the steps leading up to marriage, such as finding a suitable girl and having friends approach her family, and the marriage itself. The hope is that each individual will give equal pleasure to the other and that the families will get along.

This part of the *Kama Sutra* also discusses creating confidence in the girl after marriage, being a virtuous wife, and the conduct of husbands and wives.

5. **The role of courtesans** and how they should act.
Of course, there is no section more thorough than the verses on sexual congress itself. Making love is approached scientifically,

with the intention of finding the most desirable positions for optimum pleasure. In many cultures, the achievement of high passion may not be seen as important or even particularly admirable, but in the Indian culture it is one of three principles that must be mastered to enter the realm of "*moksha,*" or the freeing of the soul.

The three objects in life are:

1. *Dharma*: rightness, truth, and staying in accordance with proper values and religious text. (*Dharma* is the most important of the three without which the other two are meaningless.)

2. *Artha*: the gaining of possessions (from friends to material assets.)

3. *Kama*: sensual gratification.

One can well understand why the study of love has been so prevalent in Indian culture. The *Kama Sutra* acknowledges that *dharma* is the most important principle, but suggests that proper *kama* can help put one's life in alignment with *dharma* and *artha*. It is understood that attempting to master *dharma* and *artha* can lead to stress, and that *kama*, especially when brought to its highest level, can work as an antidote. According to this view, optimal pleasure allows one to be more spiritually sound and therefore can be helpful in attaining a higher level of *dharma* and *artha* as well.

As mentioned, the *Kama Sutra* treats *kama* as a science (*shastra*). It takes into consideration the many variants in partners such as the size of a man's penis or *lingam* (3 sizes), the depth of the woman's vagina or *yoni* (3 sizes), the amount of desire each person holds for the other and towards the sex act itself (3 kinds for each sex, ranging from low to intense), and the amount of time it takes a person to be satisfied. Considering these as well as other outside influences, there are a tremendous number of combinations that come together when two people make love. The different sexual positions (*asanas*) are offered to enhance the pleasure of various combinations of people.

What is truly fascinating in this work is the blending of order and science with the idea of releasing one's inhibitions during sexual congress. While positions, embraces, and markings are all named and described in detail and practice is encouraged, spontaneity is seen as equally important. The reader is advised that "the rules of *shastra* apply so long as the passion of man is middling, but when the wheel of love is once set in motion, there is no *shastra* and no order."

It is surprising to many westerners how much consideration there is for the feelings of women during love making in such an ancient writing. The *Kama Sutra* treats men and women as equal partners in love making, understanding a woman's sexual desire as equal to a man's. If the desires of both partners are fulfilled, the couple will be happy with one another and able to take their union to a higher plane.

The work of Vatsayayana and his contemporaries has survived for two thousand years, and it continues to be studied, practiced, and refined. Vatsayayana's mission was to help people appreciate the ancient art of *kama*. For many, the *Kama Sutra* may seem immoral and perversive, but it is quite clear that this collection of early writings is intended to strengthen the love of couples. As Vatsayayana explains, "This work is not intended to be used merely as an instrument for satisfying our desires. A person acquainted with the true principles of this science and who preserves his *dharma*, *artha*, and *kama*, and has regard for the practice of the people, is sure to obtain the mastery over his senses. In short, an intelligent and prudent person, attending to *dharma* and *artha* and attending to *kama* also, without becoming a slave of his passions, obtains success in everything that he may undertake."

Listen, Beloved,

the rushing wind carries

an ancient song for you.

Embrace Life

with the same embrace of love

it has given you.

And Beloved,

always remember

the sanctuary within.

"There is but one temple in the Universe,

says the devout Navalis,

and that is the human body.

Nothing is holier

than that high form.

We touch heaven when we lay

our hand on the human body."

Thomas Carlyle

VISIT TO A PLEASURE GARDEN

The woman loosened her hair, letting it tumble over soft shoulders and gave it a shake. Humming softly to herself, she lit fragrant candles and turned off the overhead lights. Scents of jasmine, rosemary, and sandalwood wafted sensuously through the air. Leaning over the bathtub, she checked the temperature and added bath gel until the water foamed with bubbly aromas. As her silken robe slipped to the floor, she glanced into the mirror and smiled appreciatively. "Yes," she thought, "I like my body." No longer the sleek lines of a girl, her full breasts and womanly hips were heaven on earth for Andrew. When she realized that he saw her as beautiful and loved her the way she was, she had begun to relax and let go of frantic and ineffective dieting.

Makalina set out an array of fragrant oils with which to anoint her body after the bath. For Andrew, she prepared Ambrosia and Raspberry Kiss—oils of love that she knew would particularly please and excite him. "I *am* a witch!" she thought, smiling. He had called her that affectionately and declared that never in his life had he experienced such passionate and ecstatic love making. He would be walking shortly into "the Goddess' Pleasure Garden," as he liked to call it, where the pressures and tensions of a demanding profession would literally melt off his bones under Makalina's loving hands. She danced a few steps across the room, letting her hips sway in time to the soft music. Her hair shimmered as she rubbed her favorite scents into the long dark strands.

She remembered how different things had been just a short while ago. When Jacques stepped out of her life so suddenly and completely without looking back—much like a person getting out of a taxi—she had been enraged and devastated, feeling utterly abandoned. Her life seemed to have come to an end. She was still feeling depressed and discouraged when she accepted an invitation from a friend who lived with her husband some distance away. Her friend had persuaded her that a change of scenery might be beneficial, but even after a week, her sleepless nights were persisting. Restlessly wandering through the silent house, she would end up in the couple's small library. Pulling out book after book to divert herself, she would leaf through the pages with little interest and inevitably return them to their neatly arranged shelves. When she encountered love stories, she had to restrain herself from flinging the books across the room and would retreat to her bed, stifling sobs of remembering.

On the night before her departure, she again found herself in the library shortly before dawn. Yawning as she ran her eyes listlessly across the rows of books, she suddenly spotted a small brown volume in a far corner. The gold lettering on the spine read *Kama Sutra*. The title sounded familiar. Leafing through the pages, she nearly banged it shut when she recognized that it contained art work from a different culture depicting lovers in various forms of embrace, their sumptuous gowns and furnishings fashioned in a far eastern style. But her curiosity about things exotic and esoteric kept her turning pages until she found herself captivated by the scope and beauty of both text and illustration.

When Makalina had been in her early teens, the concept of sex and what seemed to go on between lovers conveyed dark and mysterious secrets which she and her friends could merely guess at. It somehow felt unfair to ask her parents because they usually felt embarrassed and strained around the subject. Soon the pictures that formed in their curious young minds became tainted with the flavor of forbidden and unsavory secrets. The girls would giggle behind closed doors with a mixture of revulsion and hidden delight when older boys slipped them suggestive or explicit pictures. And then there were the inept fumblings and gropings which though somewhat exciting, were usually accompanied by a sense of shame. Gradually, the child's natural and innocent curiosity had been distorted with feelings of guilt and being bad.

Makalina sighed enviously as she continued reading about a culture which taught principles of reverence for female-male relationships and considered such training essential for young people. Appropriate conduct for men courting young maidens was defined matter of factly and with clarity and respect. Harmonious and proper gender relationships, ranging from courtship to sexual practices, promoted physical tenderness and emotional bonding between couples. This was considered vital to the well-being of a community. Ultimately aspiring to divine union, this eastern culture celebrated the principle of creation by sanctifying the rituals of a loving couple. It wedded the sacred to the profane, the spiritual to the erotic. Young girls were able to read and openly discuss among themselves what to expect from a future husband and become acquainted with practices which would later on delight them both. The book also contained discussions on the art of adornment for women along with seduction techniques which were considered important enough to depict in detail.

The next morning her friend's expression conveyed mild surprise when Makalina asked to borrow the book for a short while. She consented without asking the questions that no doubt were swirling in her mind

بهمى وهو العزيز الحكيم ذلك فضل الله

يؤتيه من يشاء والله ذو الفضل العظيم

اصفا

like birds uncertain where to alight. As it turned out, this little volume changed Makalina's life. She began to take an interest in adorning herself. Her bathroom and bedroom underwent major changes. Inspired by the art work and text of the *Kama Sutra*, she added silk cushions, soft colorful carpets, and dramatic drapes. Ornamental and fragrant plants and flowers were placed in conspicuous locations. So much of her time went into this new pursuit that the heartbreak of her last relationship soon diminished. Her playfulness rekindled, she seemed to experience a new surge of vitality. It was as if she were having an affair—with herself. "So that's what it's like to love oneself," she mused, suddenly understanding the philosophy of self love that she had heard extolled countless times.

A single woman for more than one year now, Makalina continued to relax regularly with gentle music and enjoyed her rituals of sensuous baths, lighting candles for herself, and anointing her body with precious oils. A new vivacity and radiance had begun to imbue her life. Rosy cheeks and a relaxed face belied her age, and she found herself in a good mood most of the time. "Receiving pleasure is indeed very healing," she thought as both mirror and friends reflected her improved appearance. "I wonder if more pleasure would make a happier world," she continued. Like an ink spot on white linen, this perception spread out within her mind until it seemed obvious. "That's definitely true also of small children and animals," she reflected further. "It's only us poor driven adults who sometimes forget what's good for us." She realized that fad dieting no longer fit her style. Her appetite was good and she ate in moderation. With newfound zest, she enjoyed and appreciated food in a way she rarely had before, savoring each morsel and sip with sensual reverence. Moving through her days with elasticity and easy confidence, she exuded the vitality of a healthy and well-groomed animal. Many an appreciative glance followed wherever she went.

She was thoroughly convinced that without the recent changes in her life, she and Andrew would never have found each other. Who would be attracted to a sad and lonely woman, sallow from sleepless nights? And in her mood of discouragement, how would she have responded to the dynamic qualities she had come to adore in him? They had shared many meaningful times together before she invited him to her Pleasure Garden. Since then, expanded dimensions of tenderness and delight had been opening to both of them well beyond what either had experienced before or imagined possible. "The cult of ecstasy" as it has been called, had begun to reveal its shimmering gates to them.

Makalina glanced at the clock as she finished setting out two crystal goblets for the wine they would share to launch the evening. With an approving look into the mirror, she adjusted the gardenia in her hair. The awareness of her appeal to Andrew deepened the color of her cheeks and lit up her smile, as in answer to the chimes, she flung open the doors to welcome the man she loved into her pleasure garden.

"Woman is fire, O Gautama,

her haunch, the fuel;

the hairs on her body, the smoke;

the yoni, the flame;

intercourse, the coals;

the fits of enjoyment, the sparks.

The gods offer seed in this fire.

From this offering,

man springs forth."

Brhadaranyaka Upanishad

Kama Sutra Positions

The desire to make love is deeply entwined in the fabric of all living things. For humans, it can be a playful skill, much like painting or creating music, which integrates numerous elements. A composition includes balance, texture, nuances of color and intensity, and variations on a given theme. Mastery is evidenced when the emotions of a receptive audience are touched and transformed. The same is true for the erotic arts. According to the text of *Kama Sutra*, one woman or man can creatively entertain his or her lover with countless love-making positions and keep them as engaged as if they were frolicking with thirty-two different partners. Besides contributing to variety and creating exceptional episodes of delight, experimenting with different postures of love can also provide an atmosphere conducive to intimacy and bonding. Variety definitely adds zest to love making and, by keeping boredom out of the bedroom, enlivens and extends relationships.

According to the *Kama Sutra*, when a person avoids excesses and devotes equal attention to the major principles of life, consciousness opens up to success and peacefulness. The following illustrations of sexual postures are offered as inspiration and suggestion. In experimenting, let your criteria be what feels good to both of you. Find out what sparks your fire, be creative, have fun, and include your heart. Follow one position, or all, and make up your own. Most of all—enjoy!

Contents

Listen Beloved, the rustling
Of soft cooing turtledoves
cozily pairing all night.

Come, oh my treasure, we too
Shall nestle and artfully dally
Until the prying moon departs.

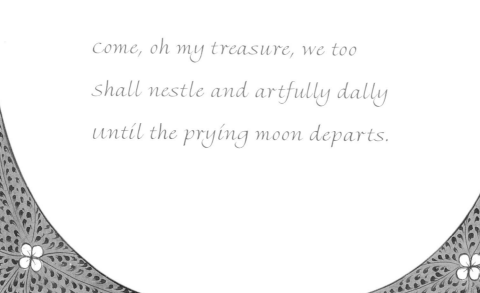

Embrace of the Jaghana

My shy little doe-eyed beauty,
where lingers your spirit today?

I shall court you with wine
And bring gifts divine
'Til your radiant smile
answers "Yes."

Rising Position

Prepare your bed strewn with
blossoms bright
Anoint your breasts with oil
For tonight we shall enter the
gates of delight
And rock on the seas of joy

Yawning Position

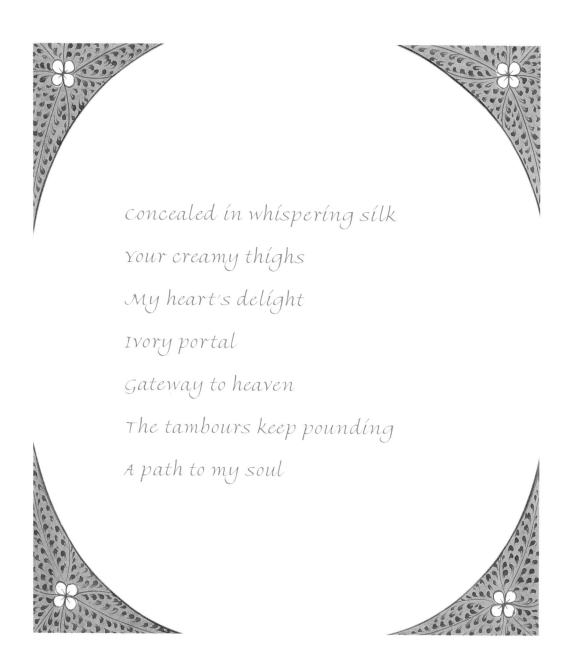

Concealed in whispering silk

Your creamy thighs

My heart's delight

Ivory portal

Gateway to heaven

The tambours keep pounding

A path to my soul

Position

You are the one I cherish tonight

My swan glides into your cave

To dally to our hearts' content

With squeals of delight

And nibbles and bites

Sampling your juices divine

I am drunk as on heavenly wine

یورپ میں بہت روشنی علم و ہنر ہے
حق یہ ہے کہ بے چشمۂ حیواں ہے یہ ظلمات!

جن کے لہو کی طفیل آج بھی ہے اندلسی
خوش دل و گرم اختلاط سادہ و روشن جبیں!

Clasping Position

Young breasts

Hot little sea shells

Melting against him

Rising to his kisses

Hands caressing

Exploring her juicy mound

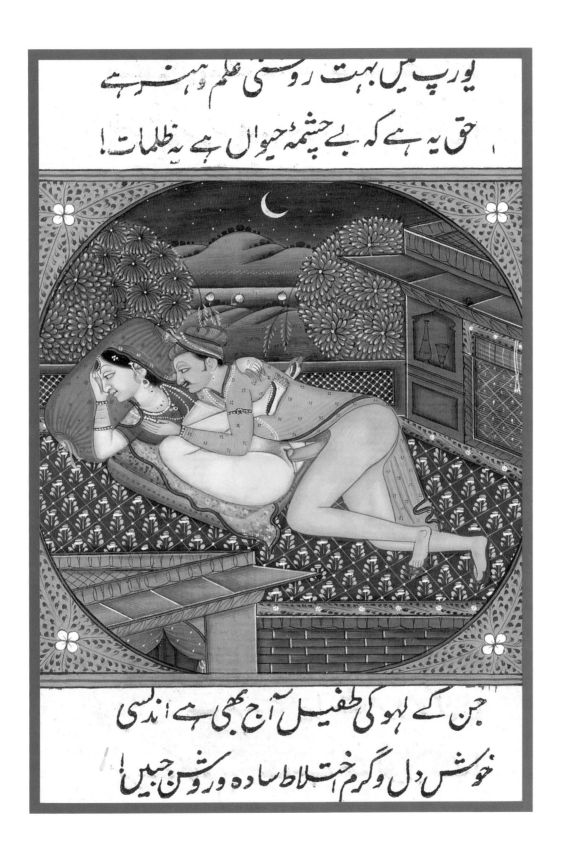

Crab's Position

My thighs a twining arbor

Enticing embraces

Deep surges of pleasure

Ecstacy

Impetuous you

Piercing Position

Stroking deeply, hotly, sweetly

My strutting peacock

fans his tail

Little red rosebud

swelling discreetly

Of our love sings the nightingale

Top Position

My fountain gushes

overflowing

Drenching

Quenching

Your scented lotus pool

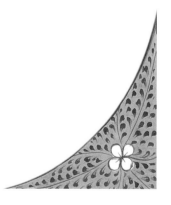

Sporting of a Sparrow

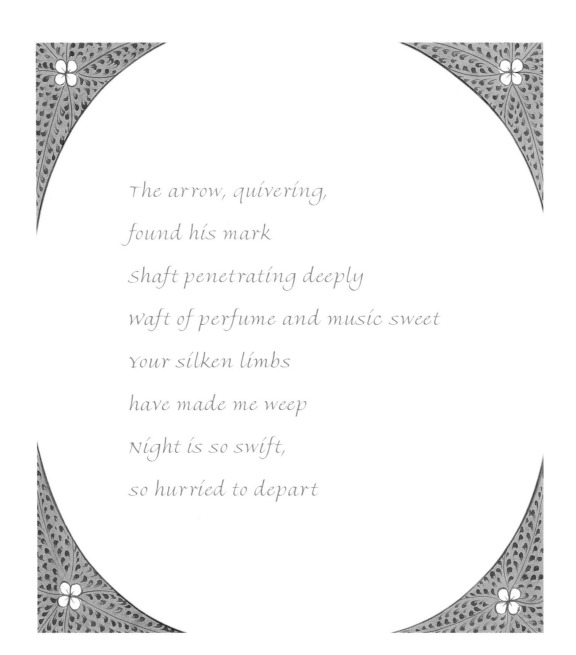

The arrow, quivering,

found his mark

Shaft penetrating deeply

Waft of perfume and music sweet

Your silken limbs

have made me weep

Night is so swift,

so hurried to depart

یورپ میں بہت روشنی علم و ہنر ہے
حق یہ ہے کہ بے چشمہ حیواں ہے یہ ظلمات!

جن کے لہو کی طفیل آج بھی ہے اندلسی
خوش دل مگر مخت اطساد و روشن جبیں!

Churning Position

Thrumming rhythms

Surging from bottomless depths

Pulsing and throbbing

Joining our bodies

Exalting heart and soul

Turning Position

Your wanton spells

Draw me into your arms

Your heady perfume

Clouds my brain

Ensnared by your magic's

Golden weave

I gladly succumb again

Lotus Position

I dreamt you were

in my arms again

Your breath caressing my cheek

Your barge slipping

into my harbor fain

And you were mine to keep

Position of Indrani

Parting your thighs

As the bow of a ship

parts the waves

Desire searing my loins

I straddle the torrid gales

Widely Opened Position

I cast into your lotus pool
My hard-tipped angling rod.

Come, oh beloved,
worshipful,
I clasp you to my heart.

Splitting of a Bamboo

Rash as a fiery stallion

He breached her welcoming gates

Muffled her little cries of delight

With kisses of flaming desire

Til soaring and melting

Hearts thundered as one

میرود جهہ غم است پہ دربہ بند دجنانکہ یک پہ کر دل از عمر بر کند
شاید پہ ورکشاید جنانکہ توان لیبت پہ کو بشواز حیات دنیا سیت

بود ود رحبرہ ہم جلیس برسم قدیم از دردر آمد جنانکہ نشاط ملاعیت

Packed Position

Sweet love,

I thank God for the gift of you

And the journey of joy

I take when I look into

Your liquid eyes.

Sitting Position

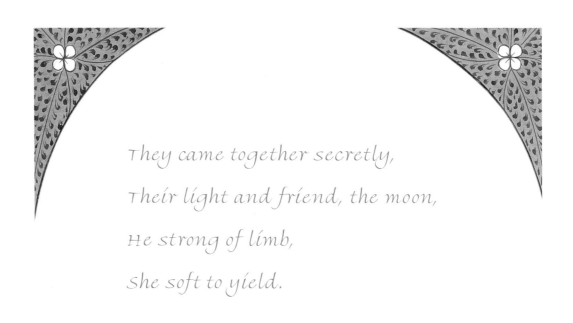

They came together secretly,
Their light and friend, the moon,
He strong of limb,
She soft to yield.

Whispering love,
Their hips entwined,
Melting time in hot embrace,
Night passed all too soon.

Suspended Congress

Desire swells like a symphony

Your beauty enraptures my soul

Sensuous beings

Powerful feelings

Wanton-eyed temptress of mine

Supported Congress

"In the embrace of his beloved

a man forgets the whole world—

everything both within and without.

In the same way,

he who embraces the Self

knows neither within

nor without."

upanishad

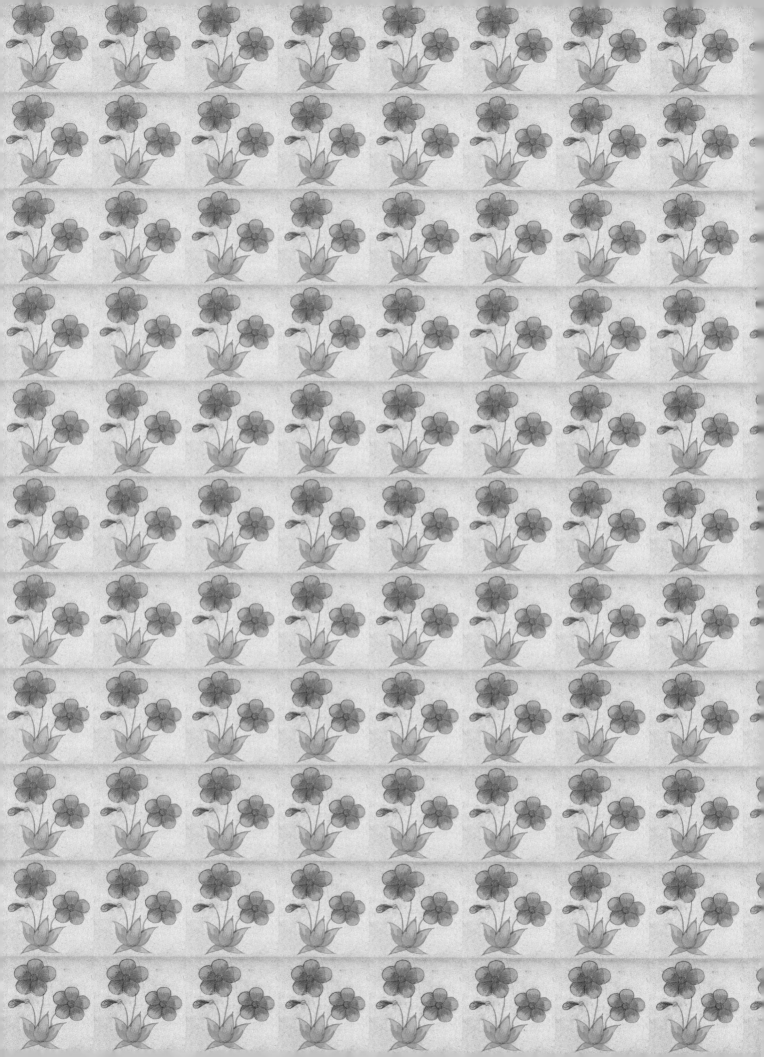